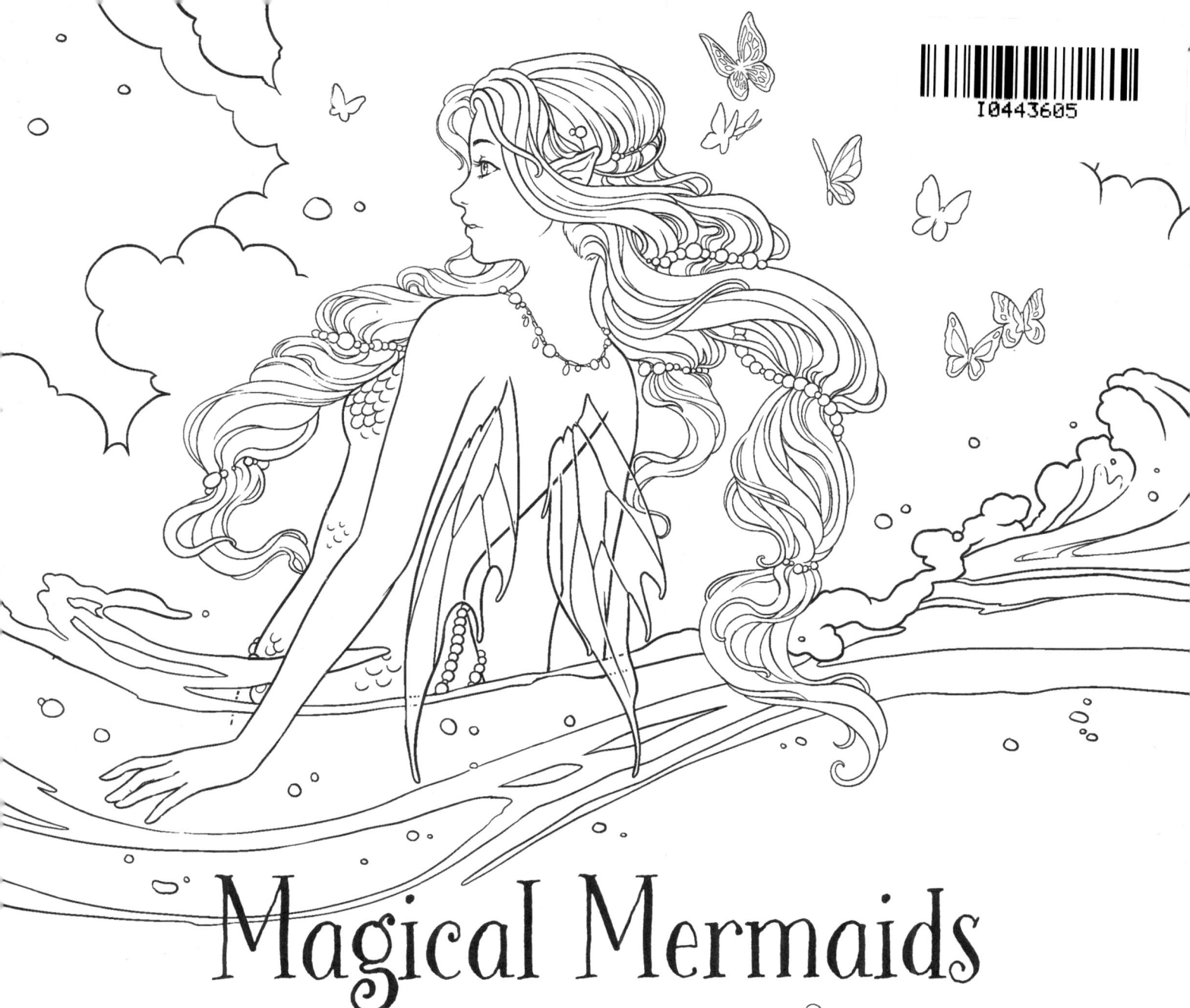

Magical Mermaids
Coloring book by Meredith Dillman

This book is a collection of my mermaid illustrations chosen from artwork spanning over ten years of my career. Older drawings have been specially updated for this book. My mermaids are inspired by aquatic animals like jellyfish, Koi, Betta fish and sea slugs; and also butterflies, flowers, and historical fashions. Each artwork is based on one of my finished ink and watercolor paintings. I hope you will enjoy bringing them to life by adding color!

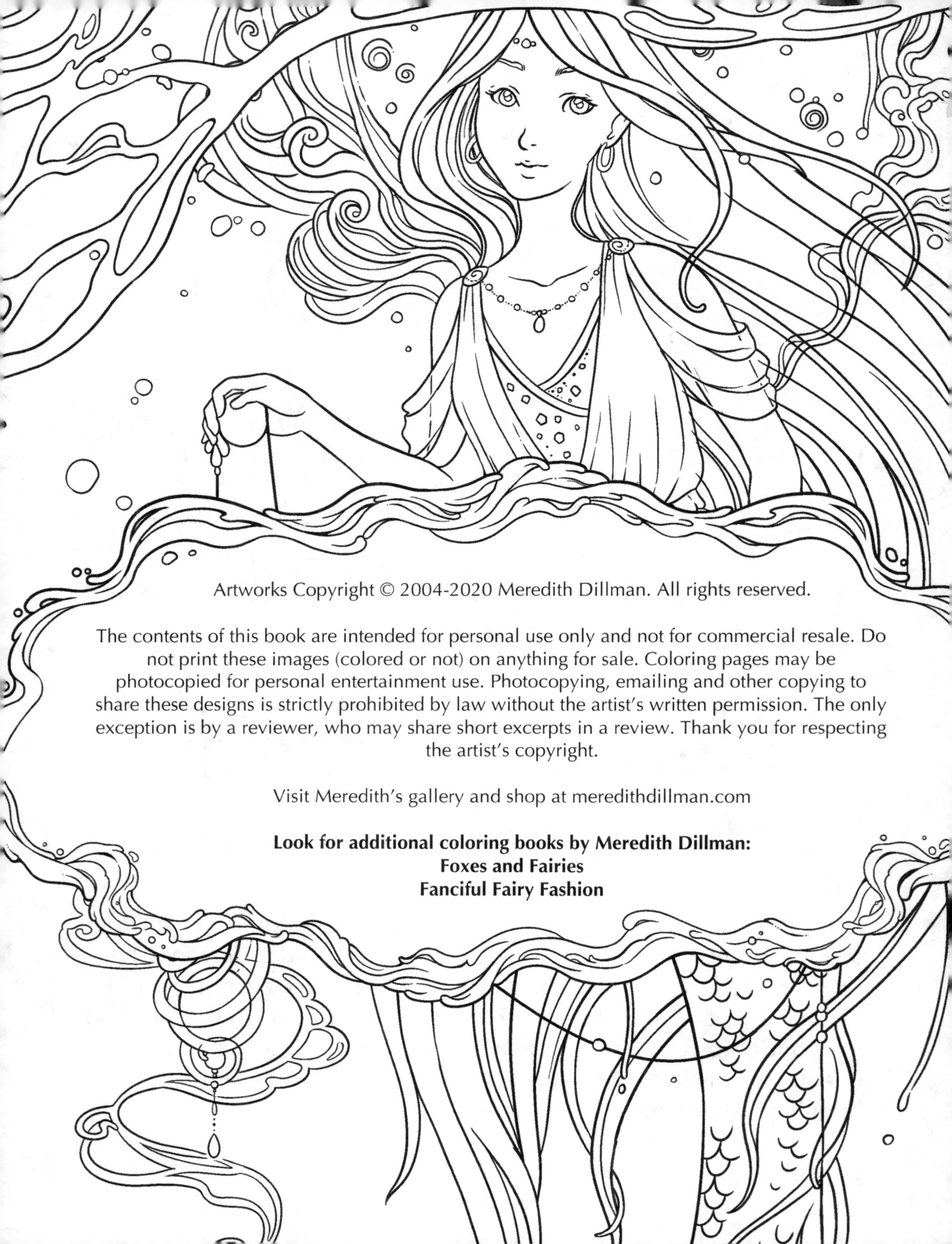

Artworks Copyright © 2004-2020 Meredith Dillman. All rights reserved.

The contents of this book are intended for personal use only and not for commercial resale. Do not print these images (colored or not) on anything for sale. Coloring pages may be photocopied for personal entertainment use. Photocopying, emailing and other copying to share these designs is strictly prohibited by law without the artist's written permission. The only exception is by a reviewer, who may share short excerpts in a review. Thank you for respecting the artist's copyright.

Visit Meredith's gallery and shop at meredithdillman.com

**Look for additional coloring books by Meredith Dillman:
Foxes and Fairies
Fanciful Fairy Fashion**

How to use this book

- Use color pencils, markers or a combination with this book. Gel pens and glitter pens make great accents too.

- Images are printed on one side only. The paper is not bleed-proof, so please place a heavy piece of paper or few sheets of copy paper under each page to avoid bleed through or indentations on other pages.

- Most importantly, have fun and relax! Enjoy bringing each image to life with your own color choices. Remember that no color combination is wrong and experimentation is fine. Nothing in art needs to be the color we expect it to be in real life.

- If you post your colored versions online, please credit Meredith Dillman and link to meredithdillman.com - Thank you!

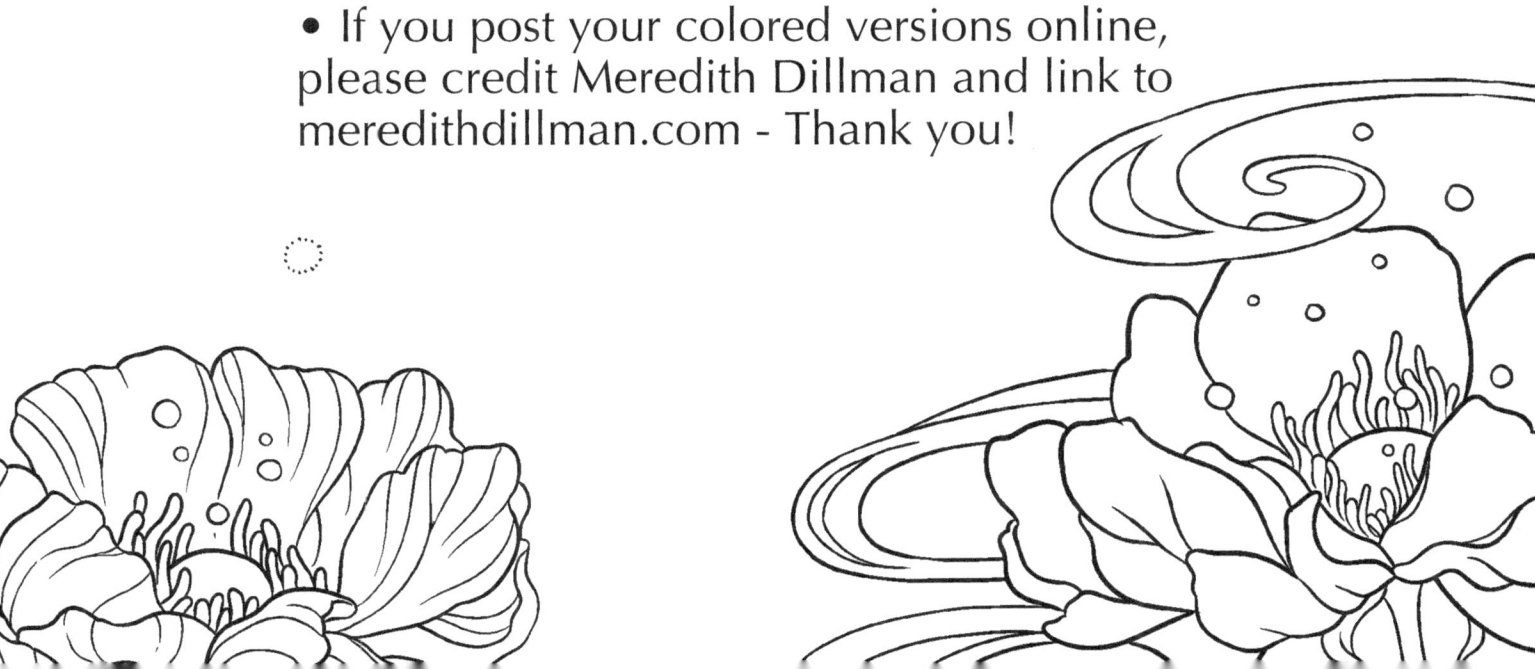

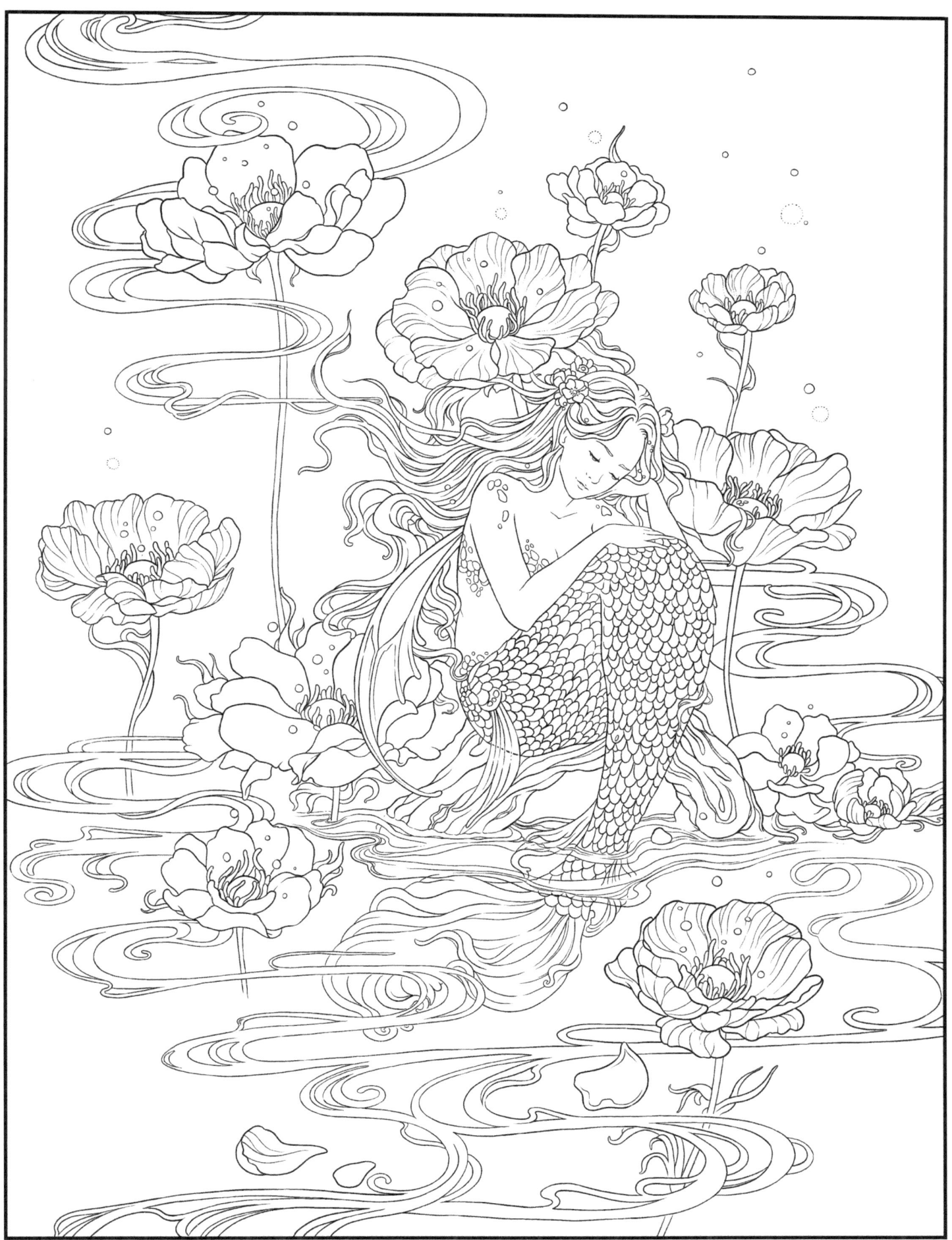

Previous Page: The Luminous Depths
Lineart by Meredith Dillman

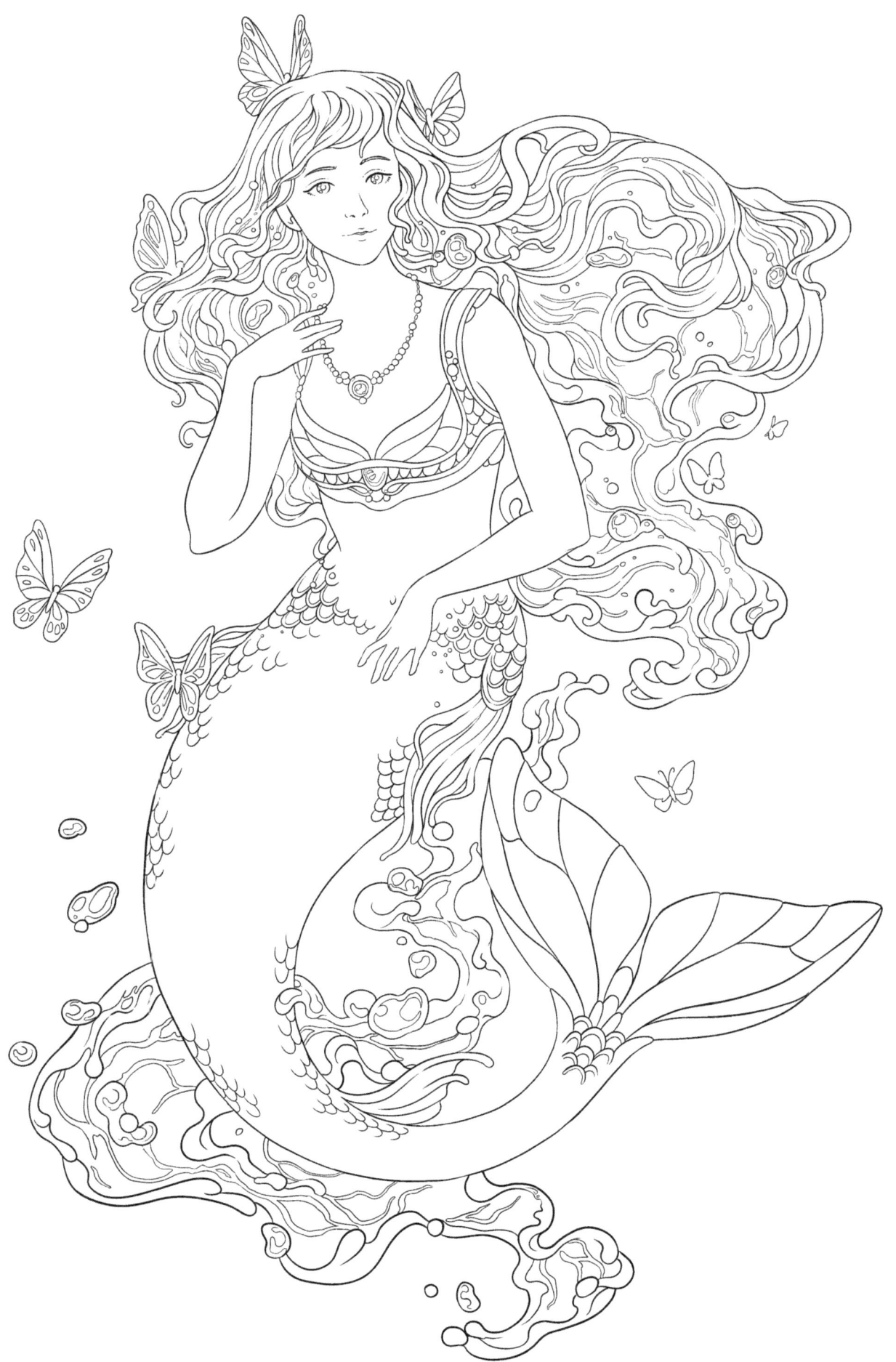

Previous Page: Blue Mermaid
Lineart by Meredith Dillman

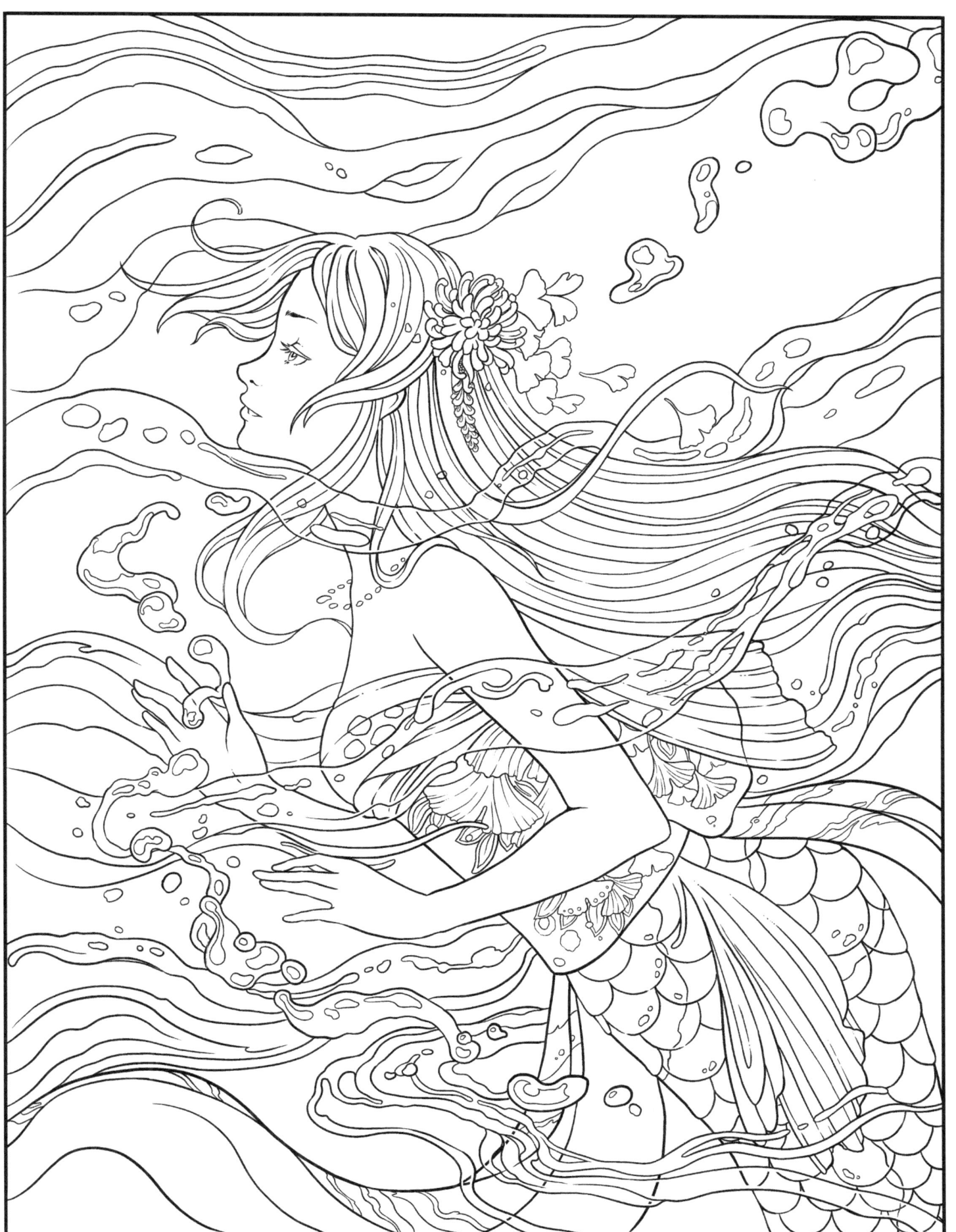

Previous Page: A Koi Mermaid
Lineart by Meredith Dillman

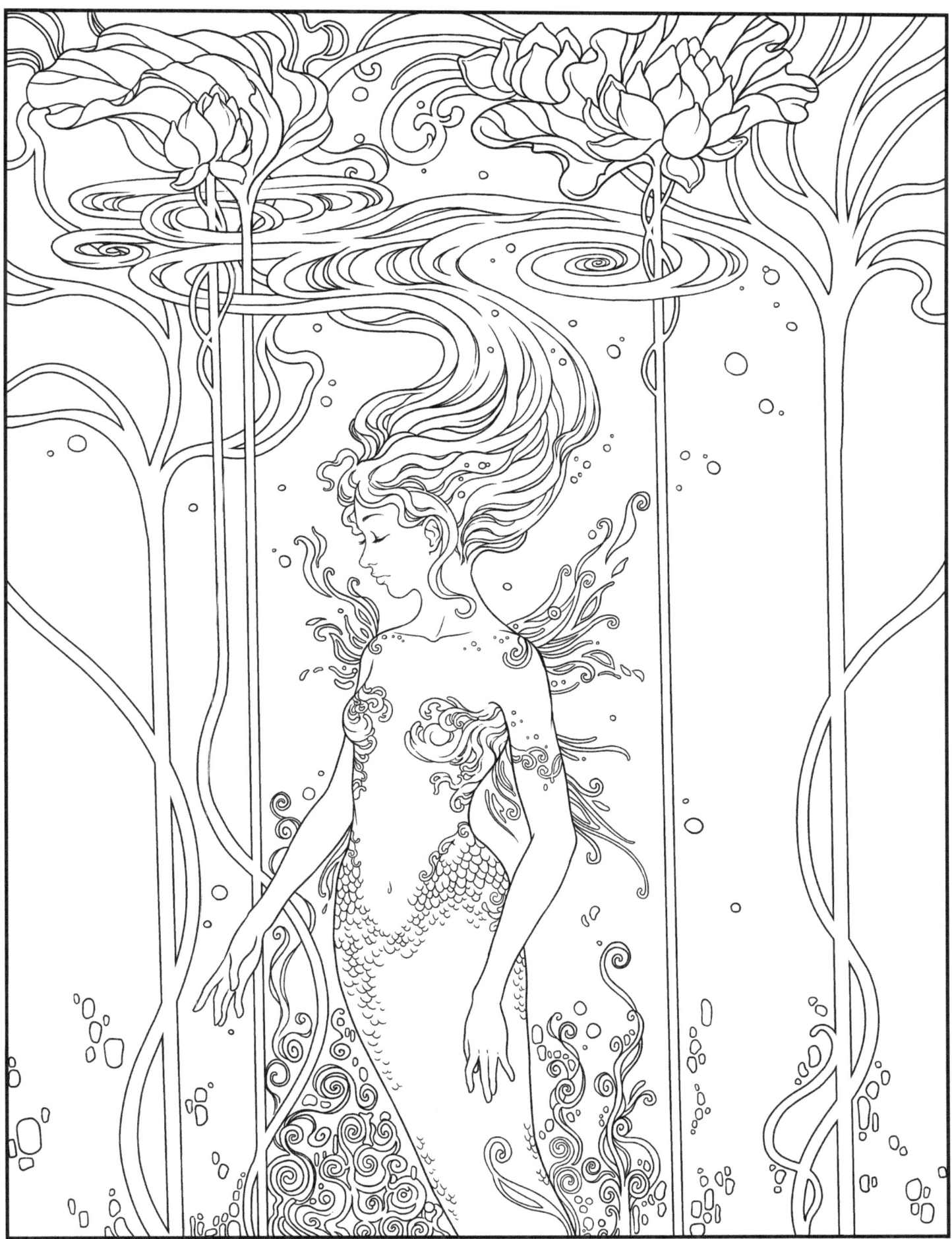

Previous Page: Lotus Mermaid
Lineart by Meredith Dillman

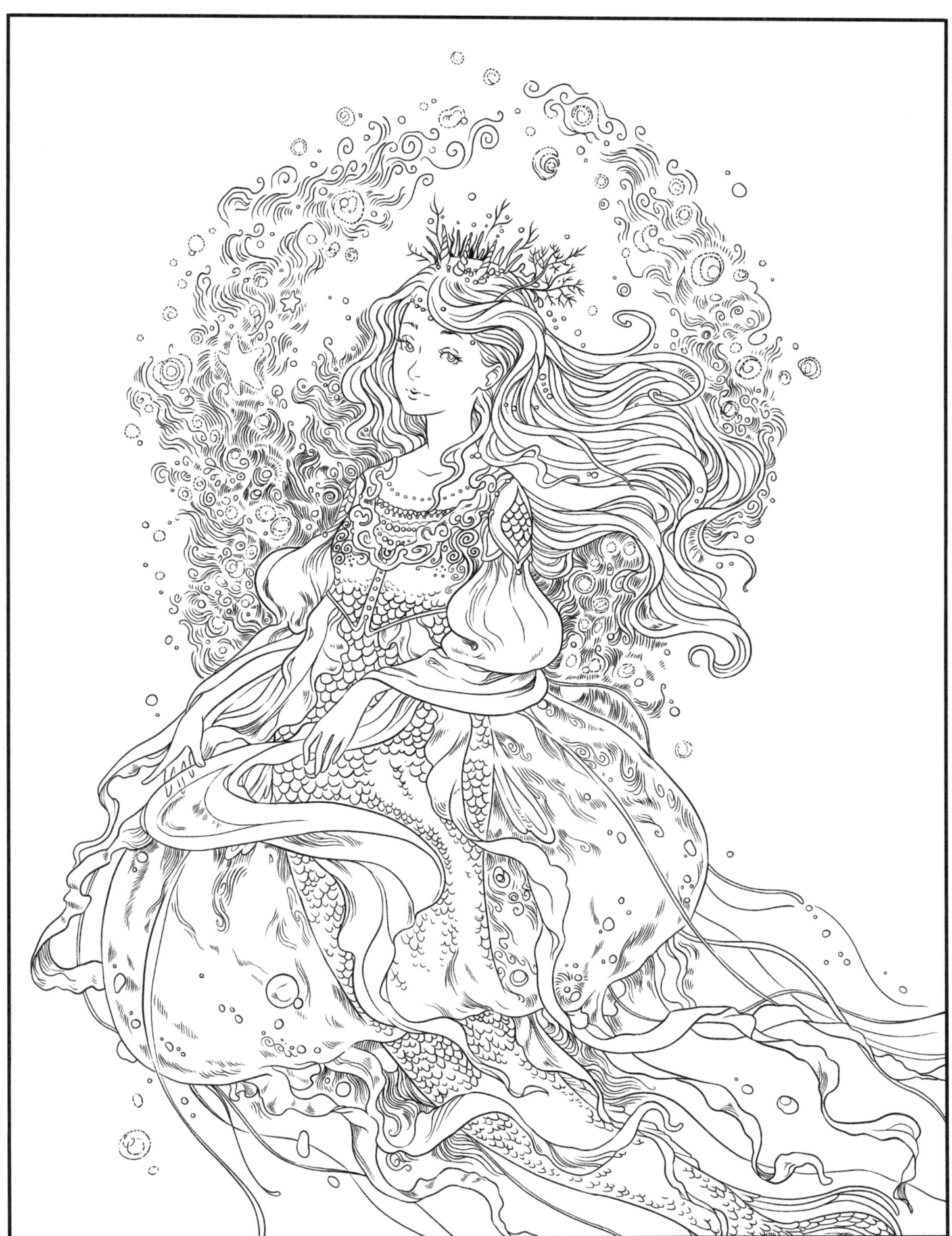

Previous Page: Jellyfish Dress
Lineart by Meredith Dillman

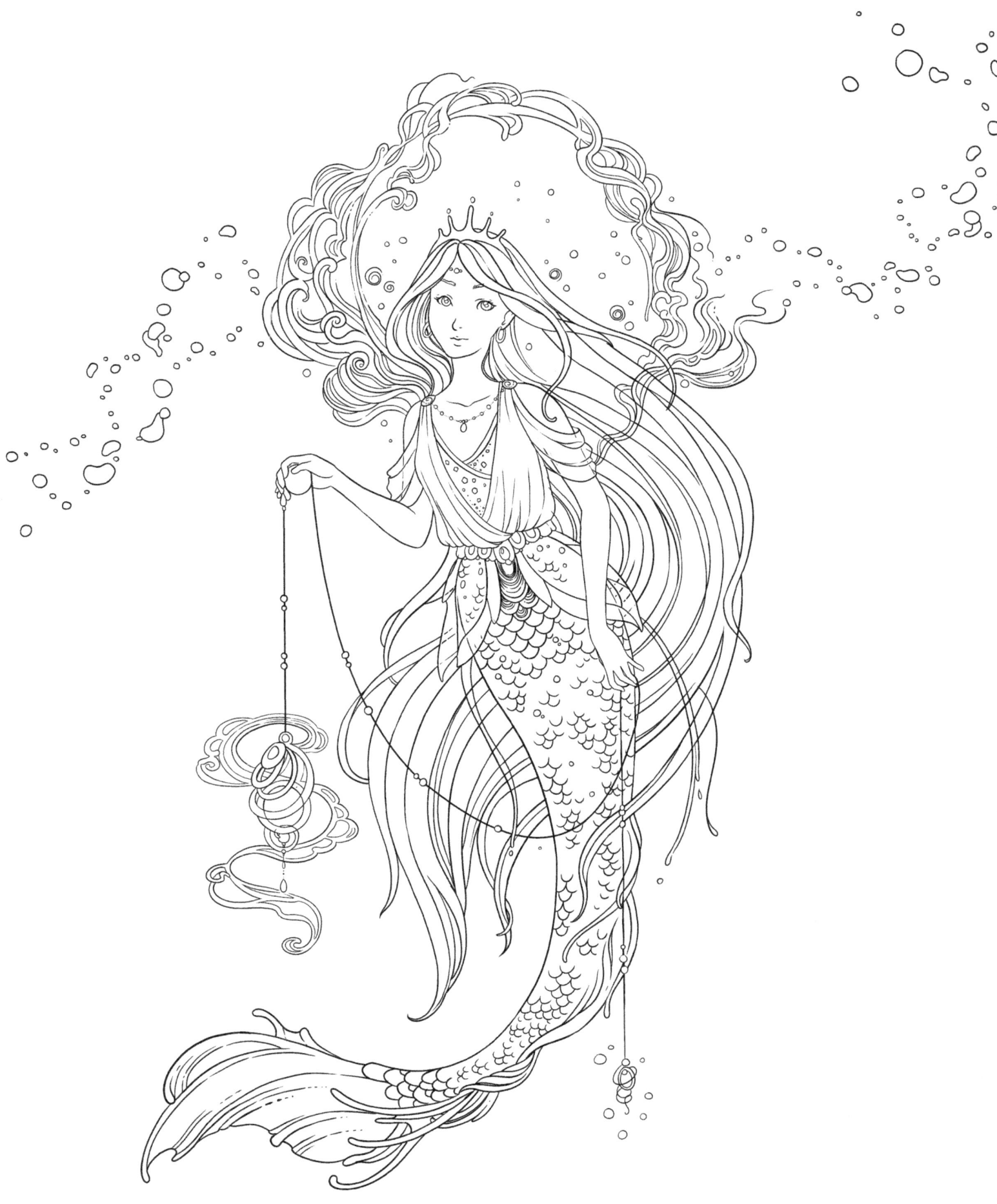

Previous Page: Lamp Bearer
Lineart by Meredith Dillman

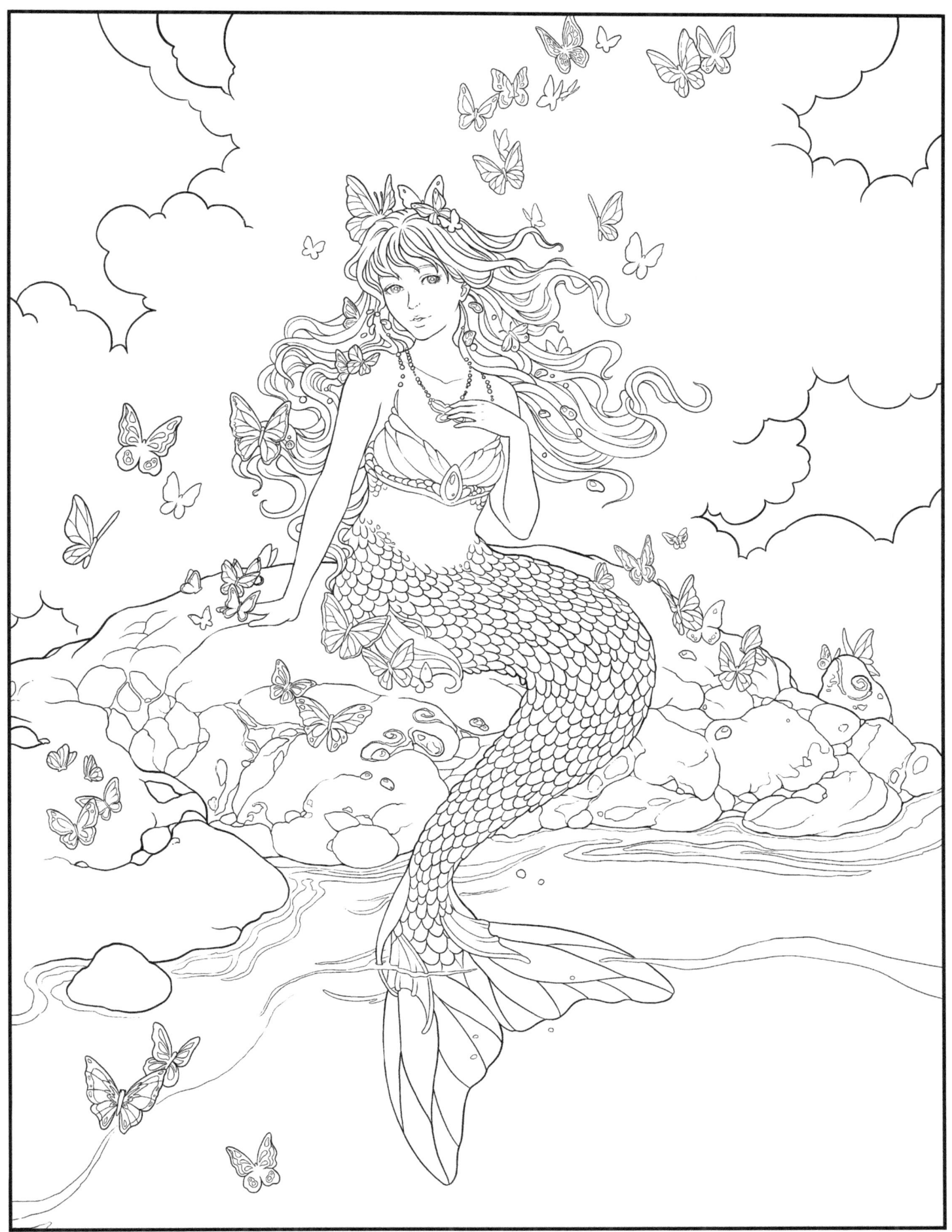

Previous Page: Blue Morpho
Lineart by Meredith Dillman

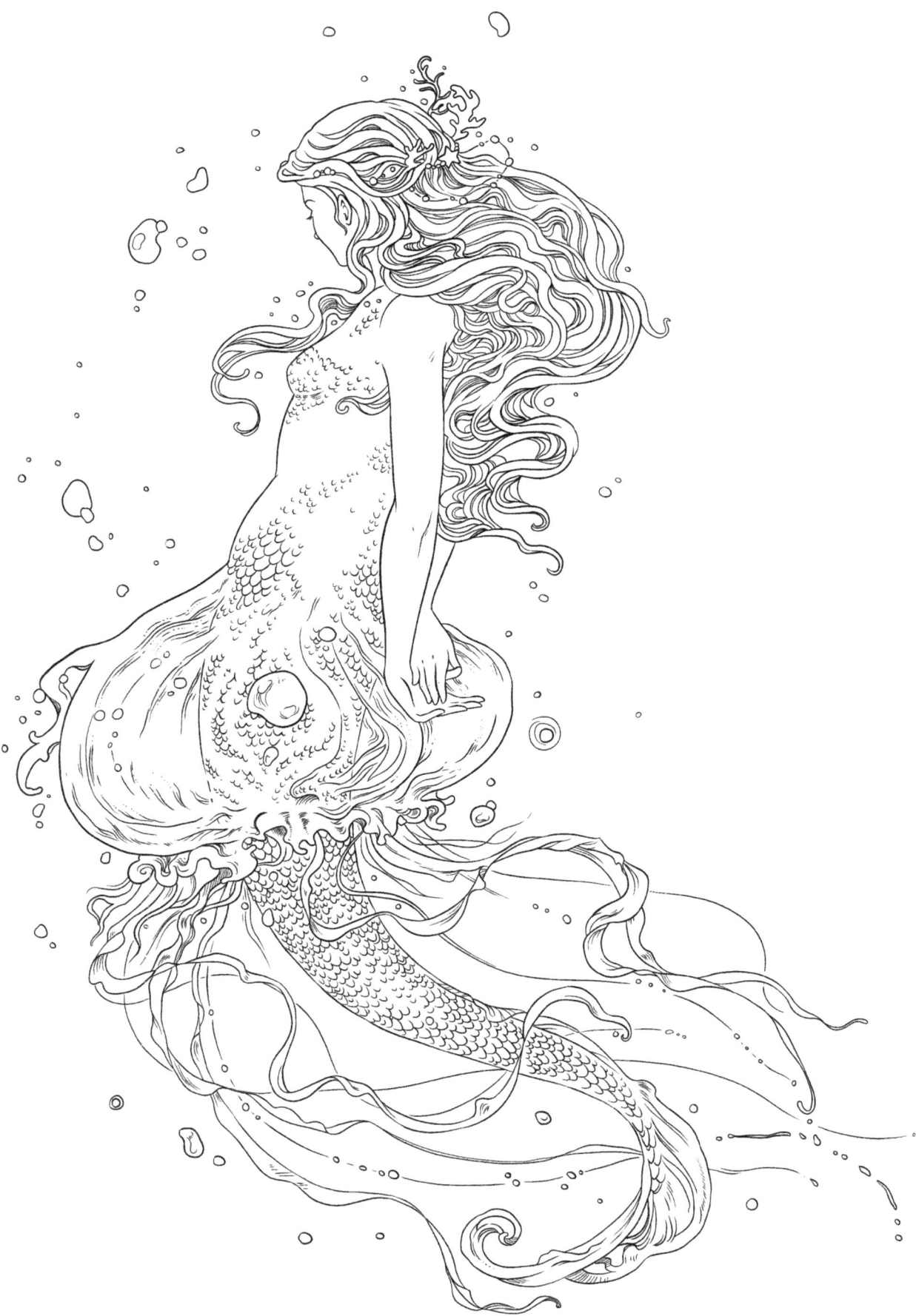

Previous Page: Jellyfish Mermaid
Lineart by Meredith Dillman

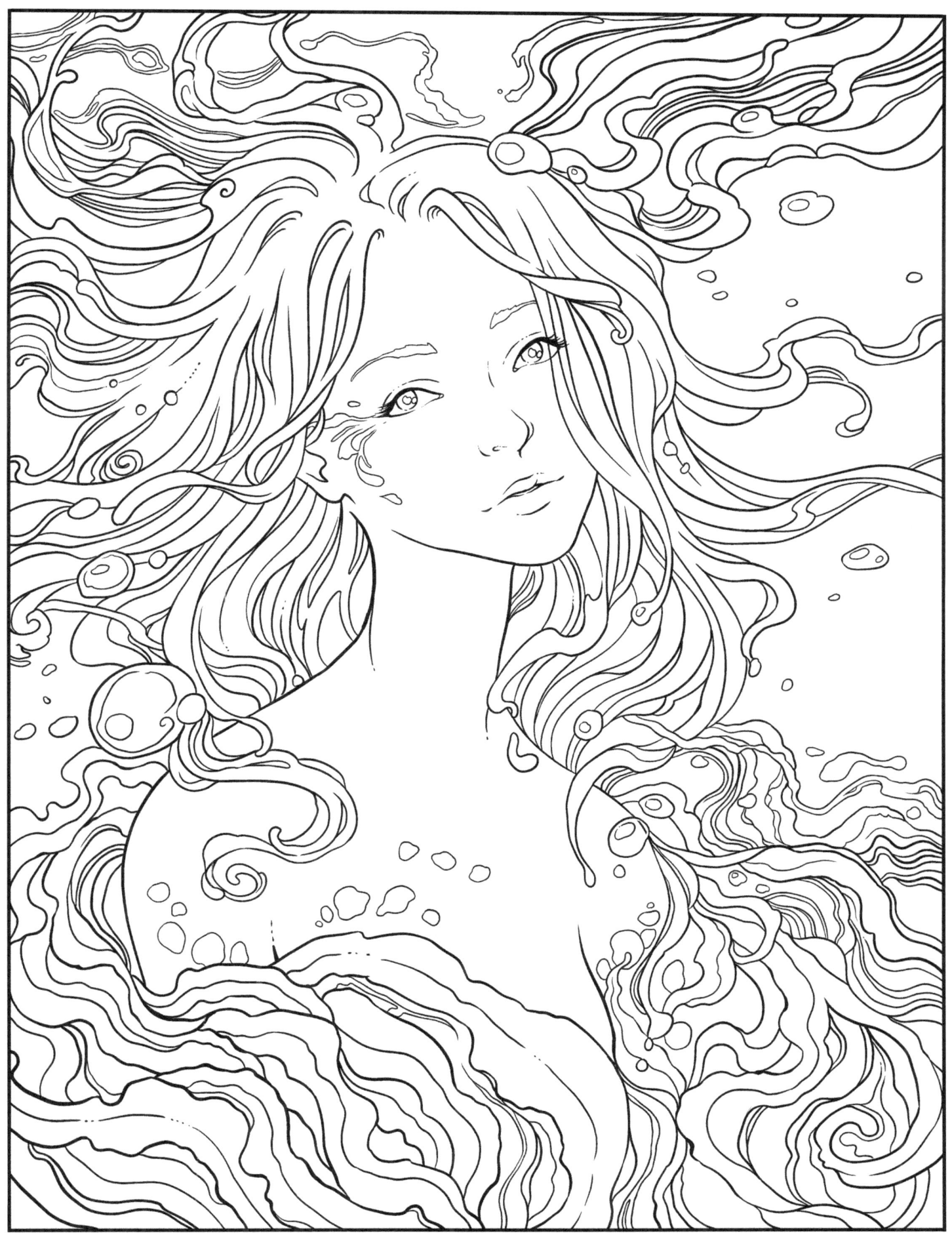

Previous Page: A Watery Portrait
Lineart by Meredith Dillman

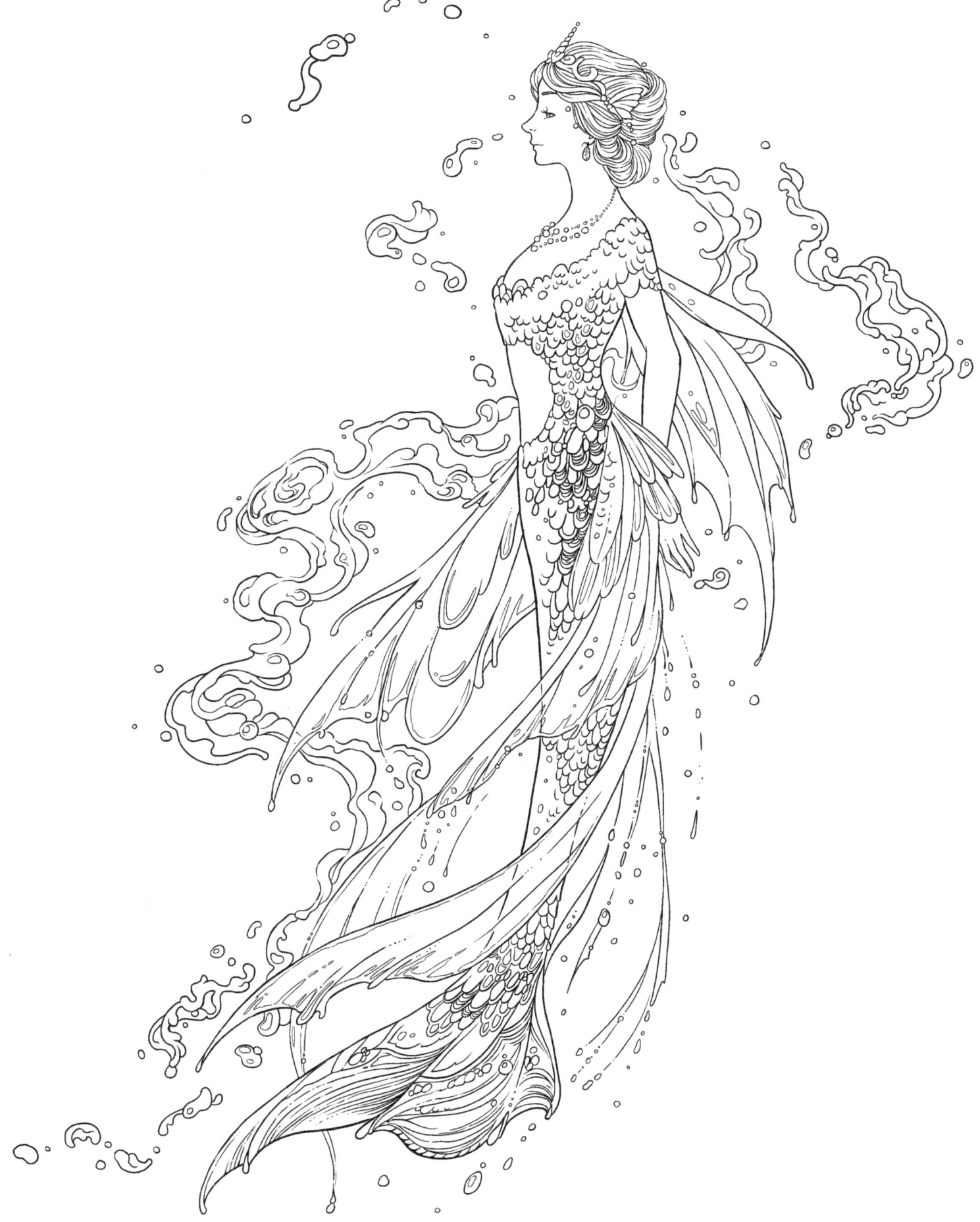

Previous Page: Art Deco Mermaid
Lineart by Meredith Dillman

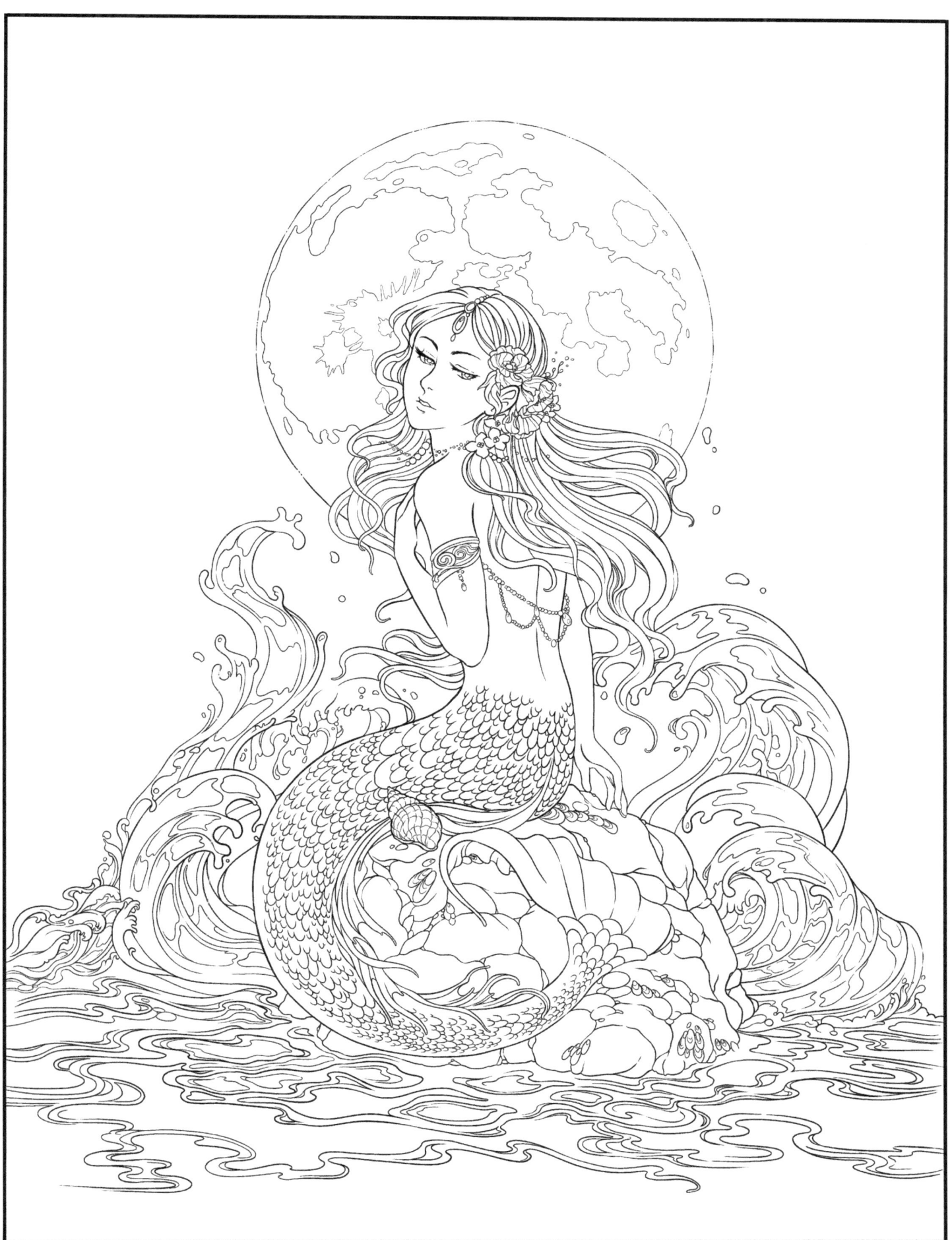

Previous Page: Moon Mermaid
Lineart by Meredith Dillman

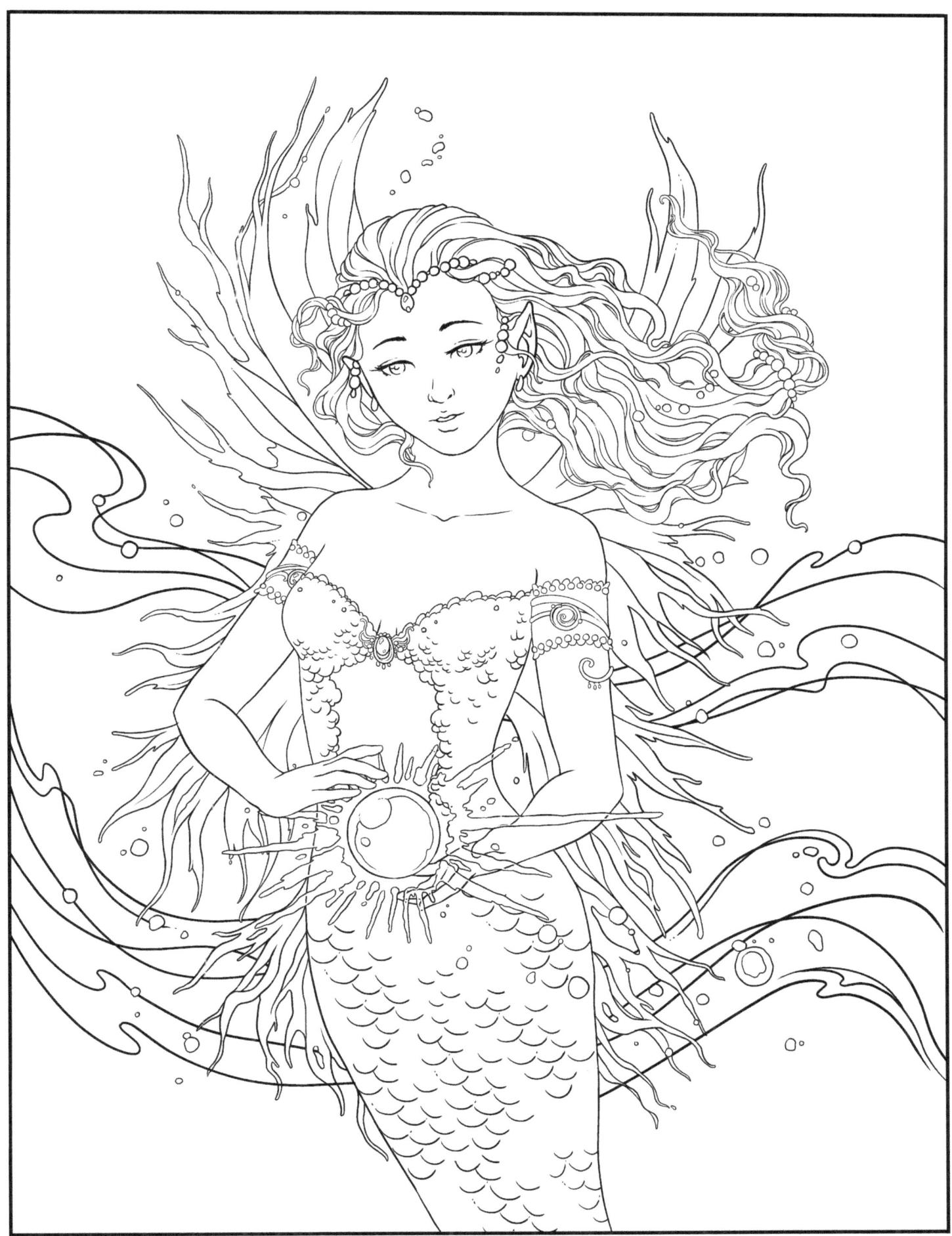

Previous Page: Pearl
Lineart by Meredith Dillman

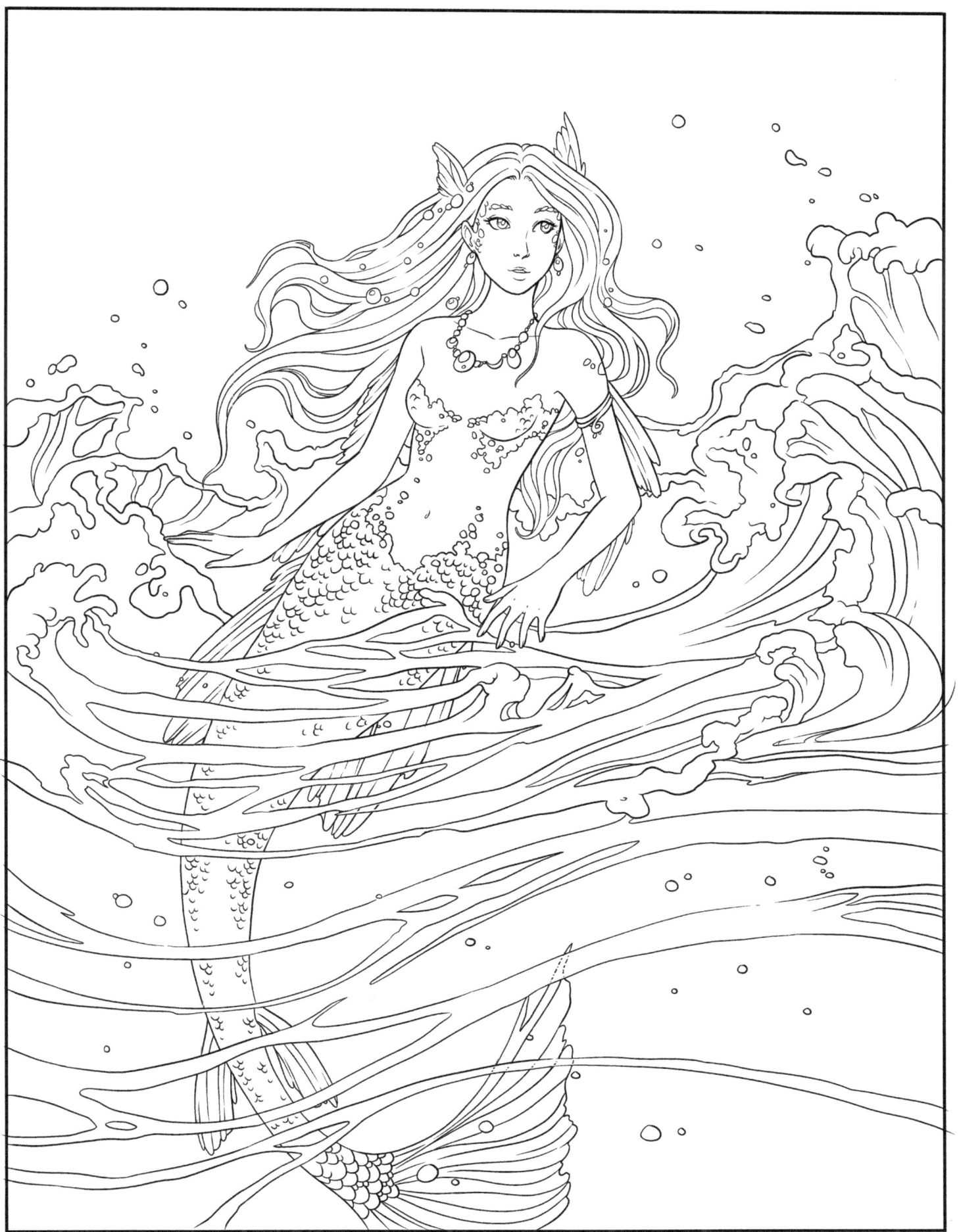

Previous Page: Ocean Waves
Lineart by Meredith Dillman

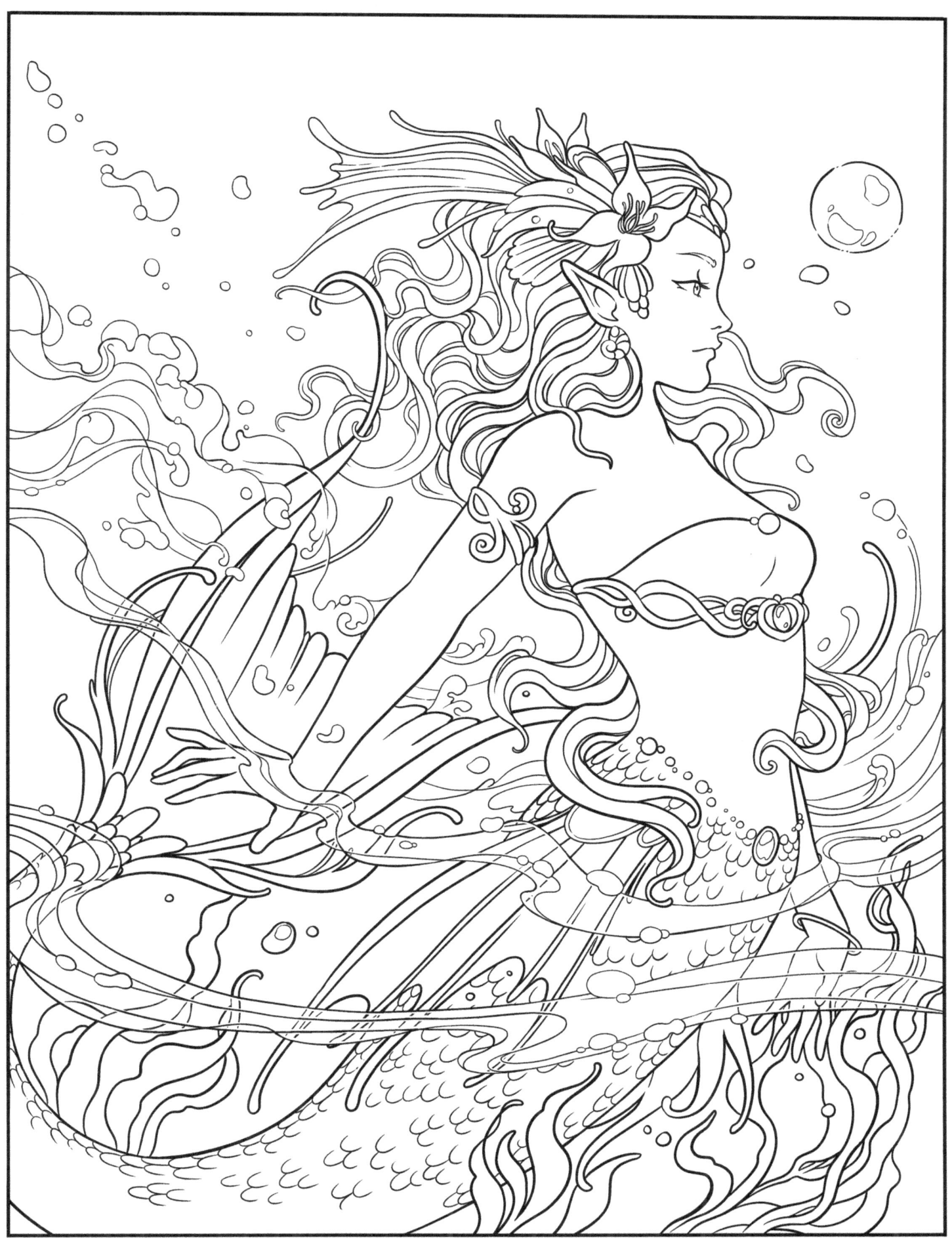

Previous Page: Seaweed Mermaid
Lineart by Meredith Dillman

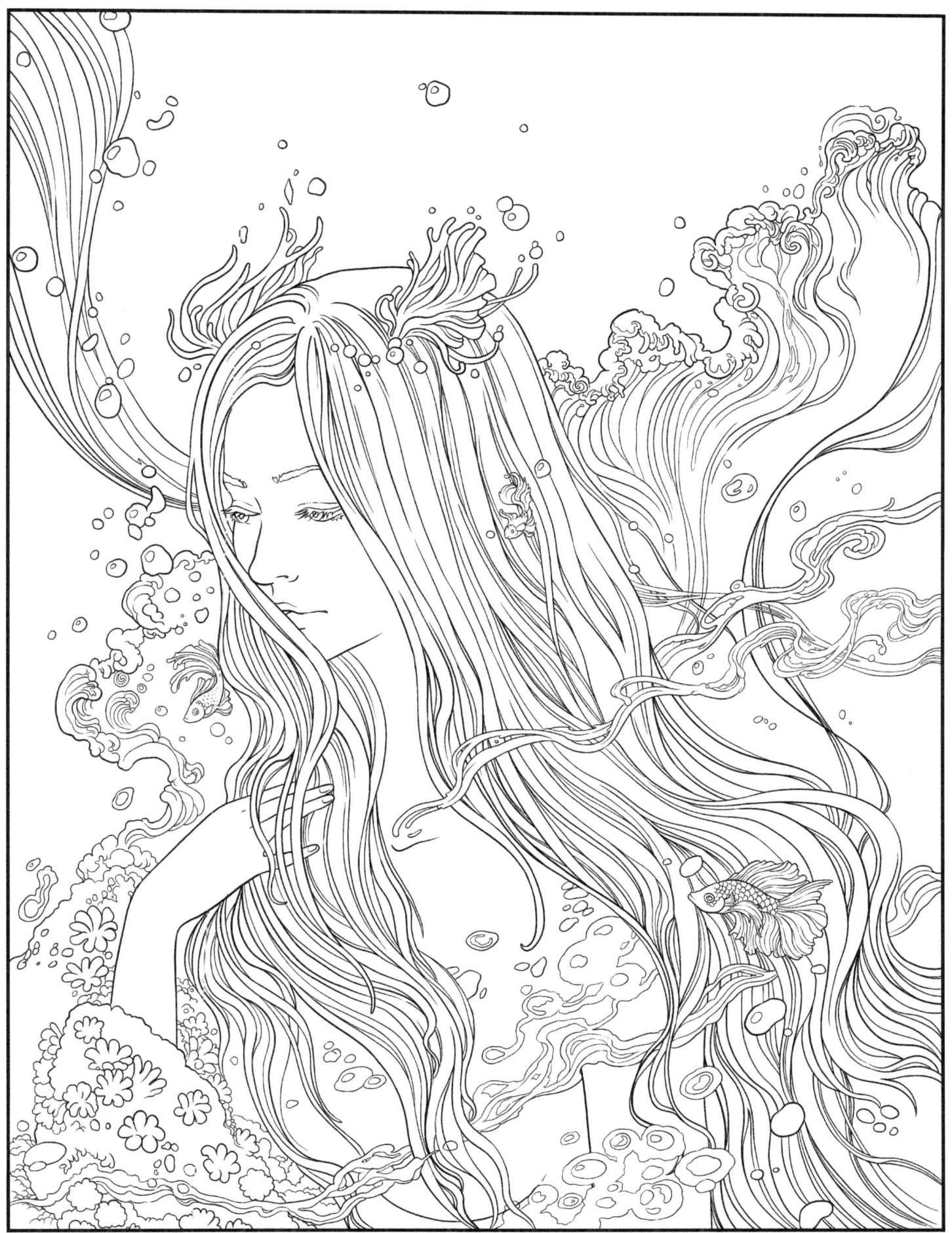

Previous Page: Blue
Lineart by Meredith Dillman

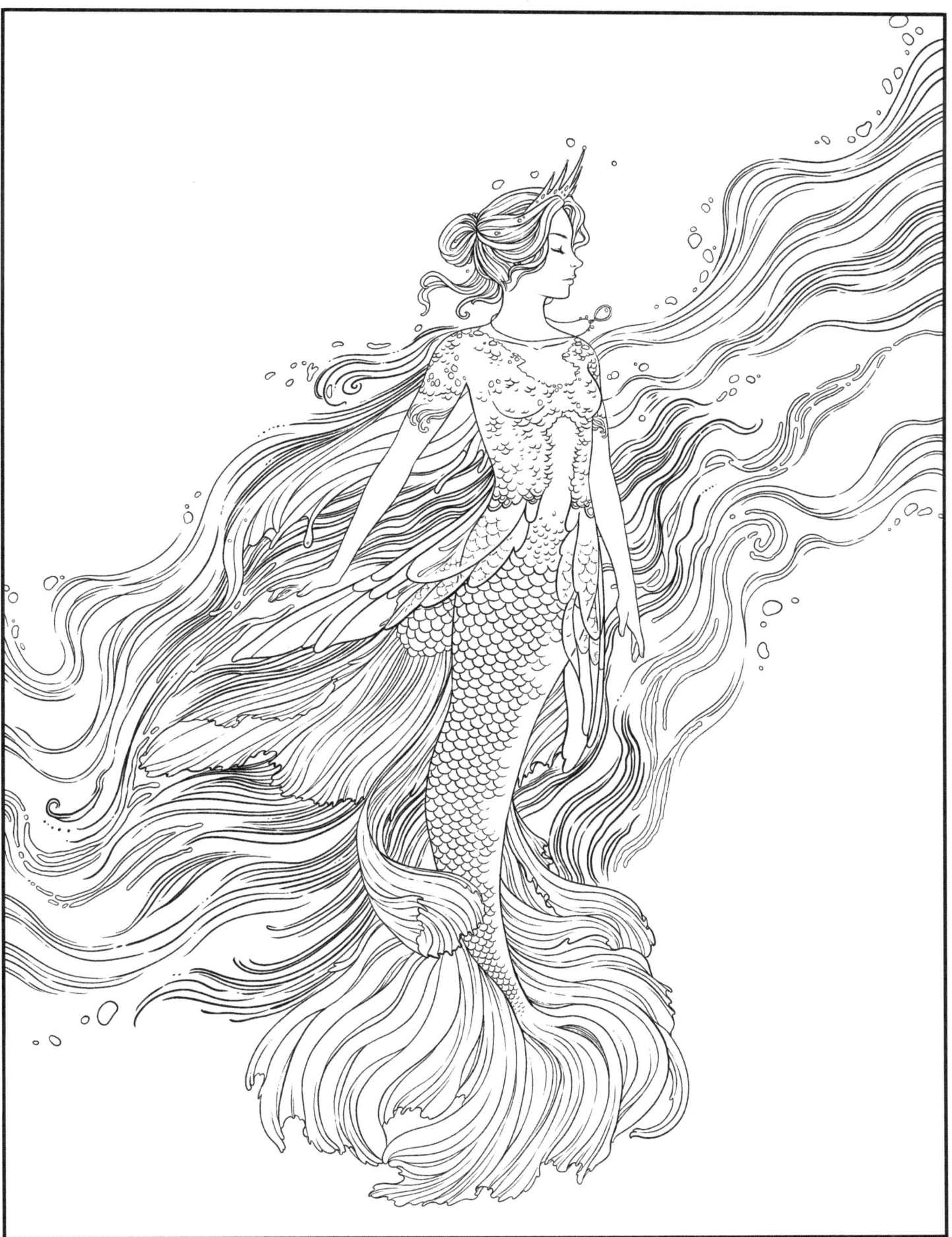

Previous Page: Betta Mermaid
Lineart by Meredith Dillman

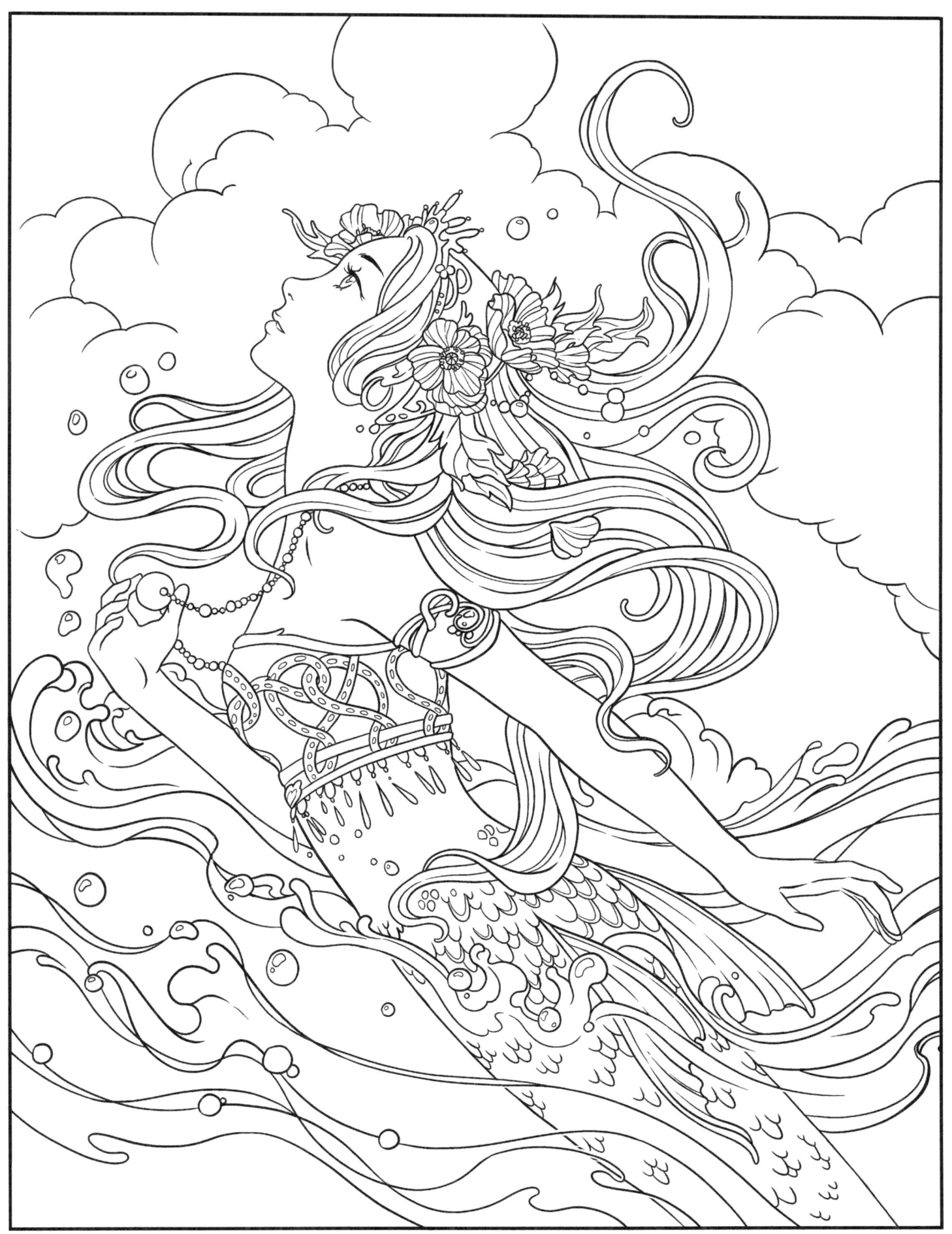

Previous Page: Poppies
Lineart by Meredith Dillman

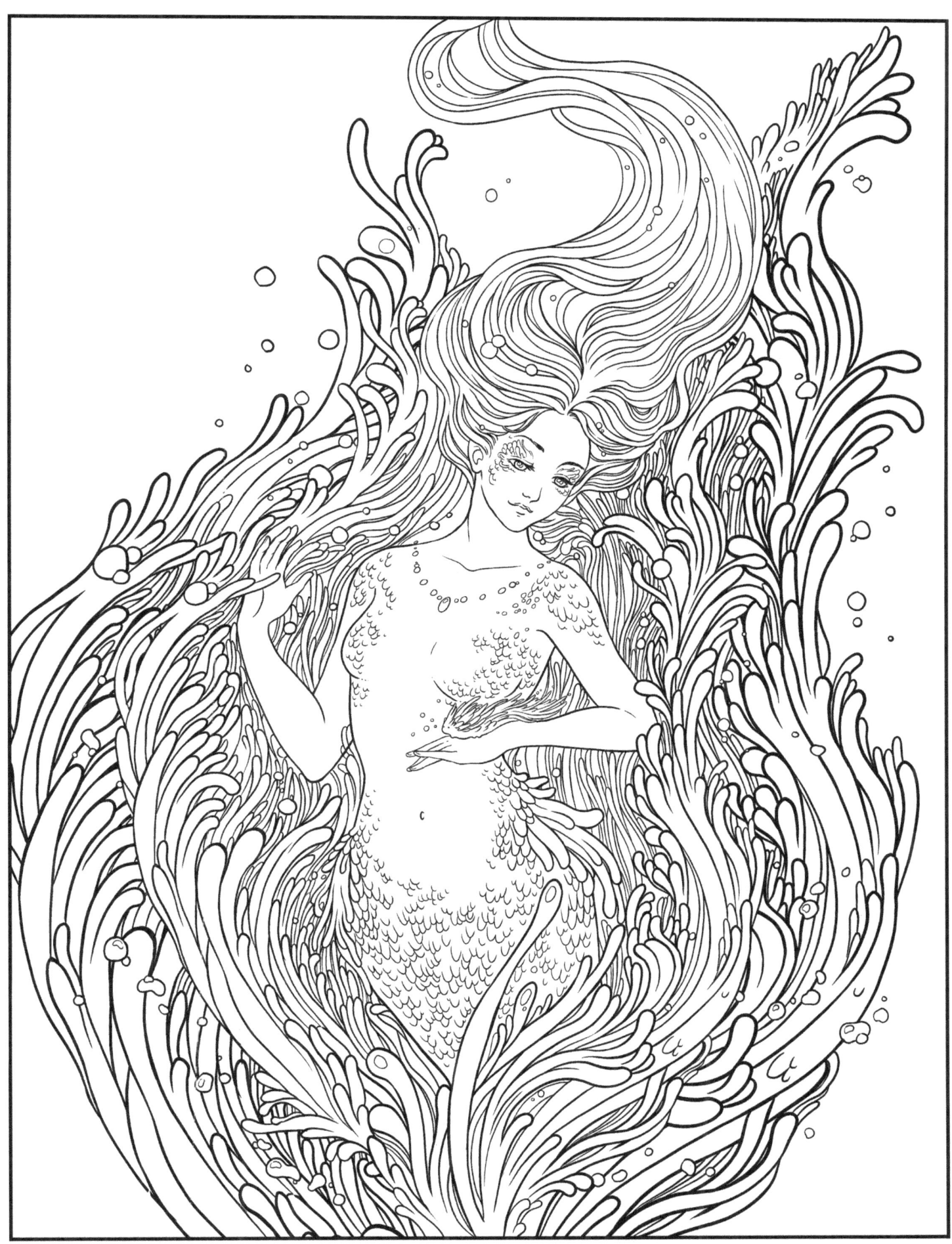

Previous Page: Mermaid with Sea Slug
Lineart by Meredith Dillman

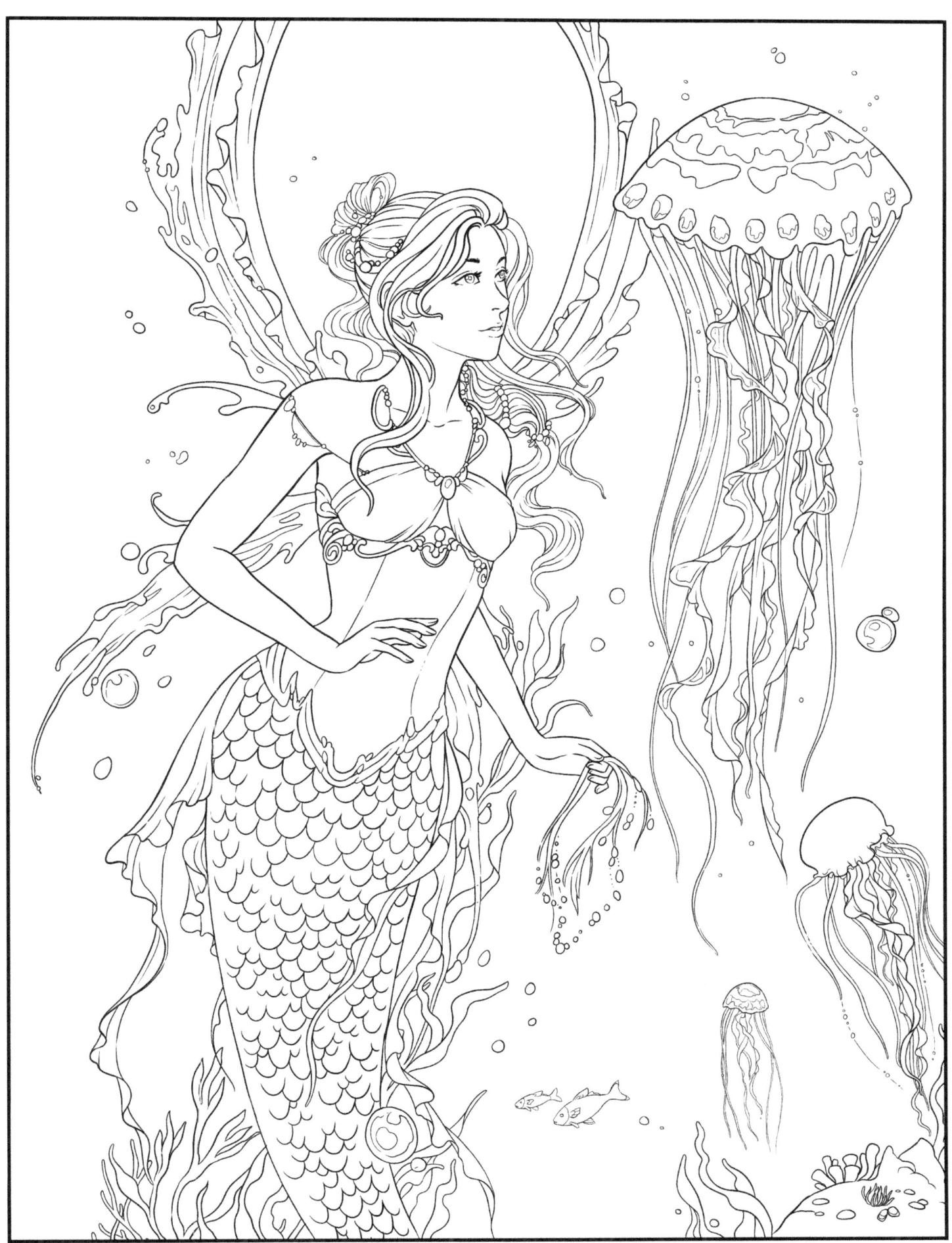

Previous Page: Curiosity
Lineart by Meredith Dillman

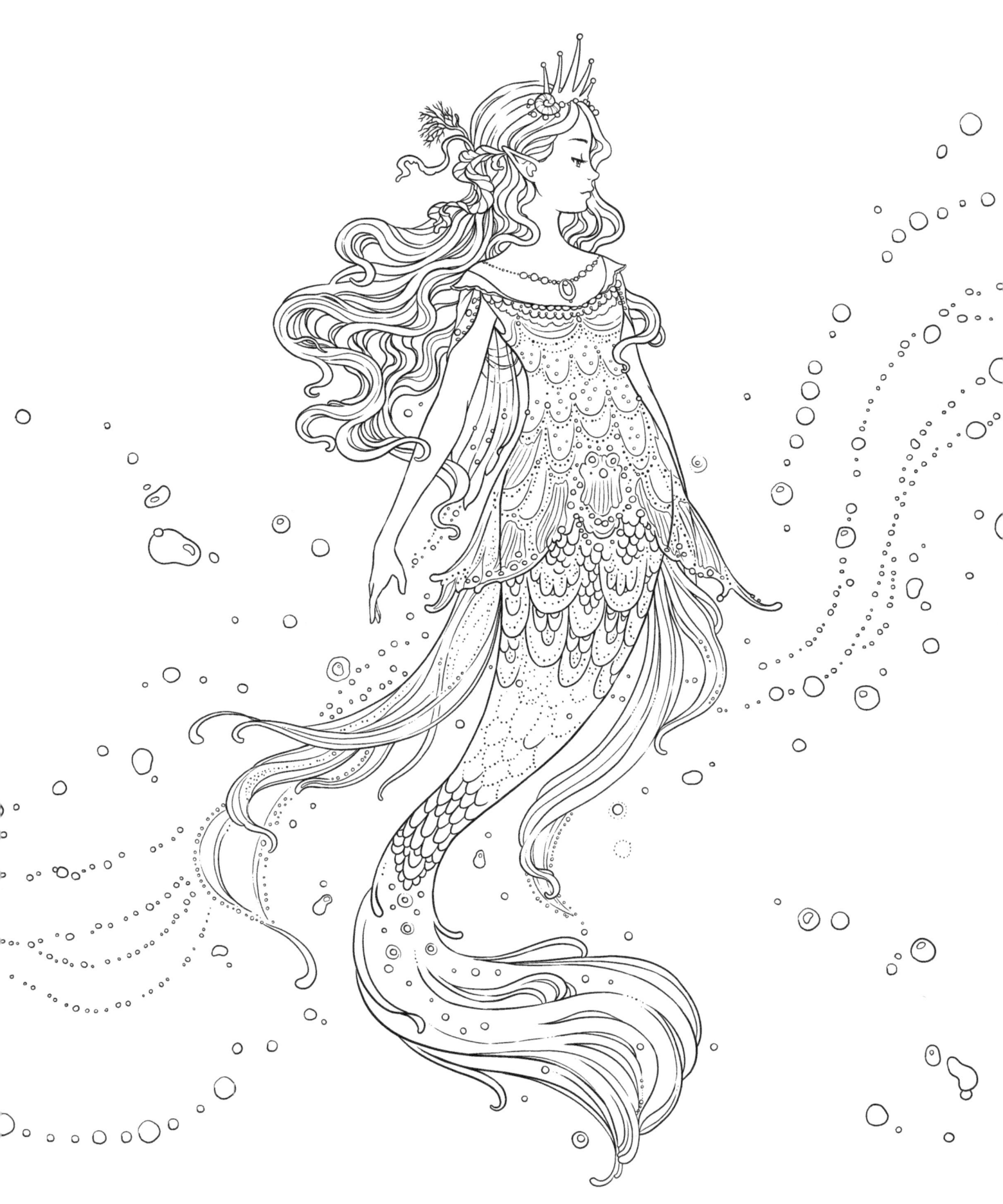

Previous Page: Art Deco Mermaid
Lineart by Meredith Dillman

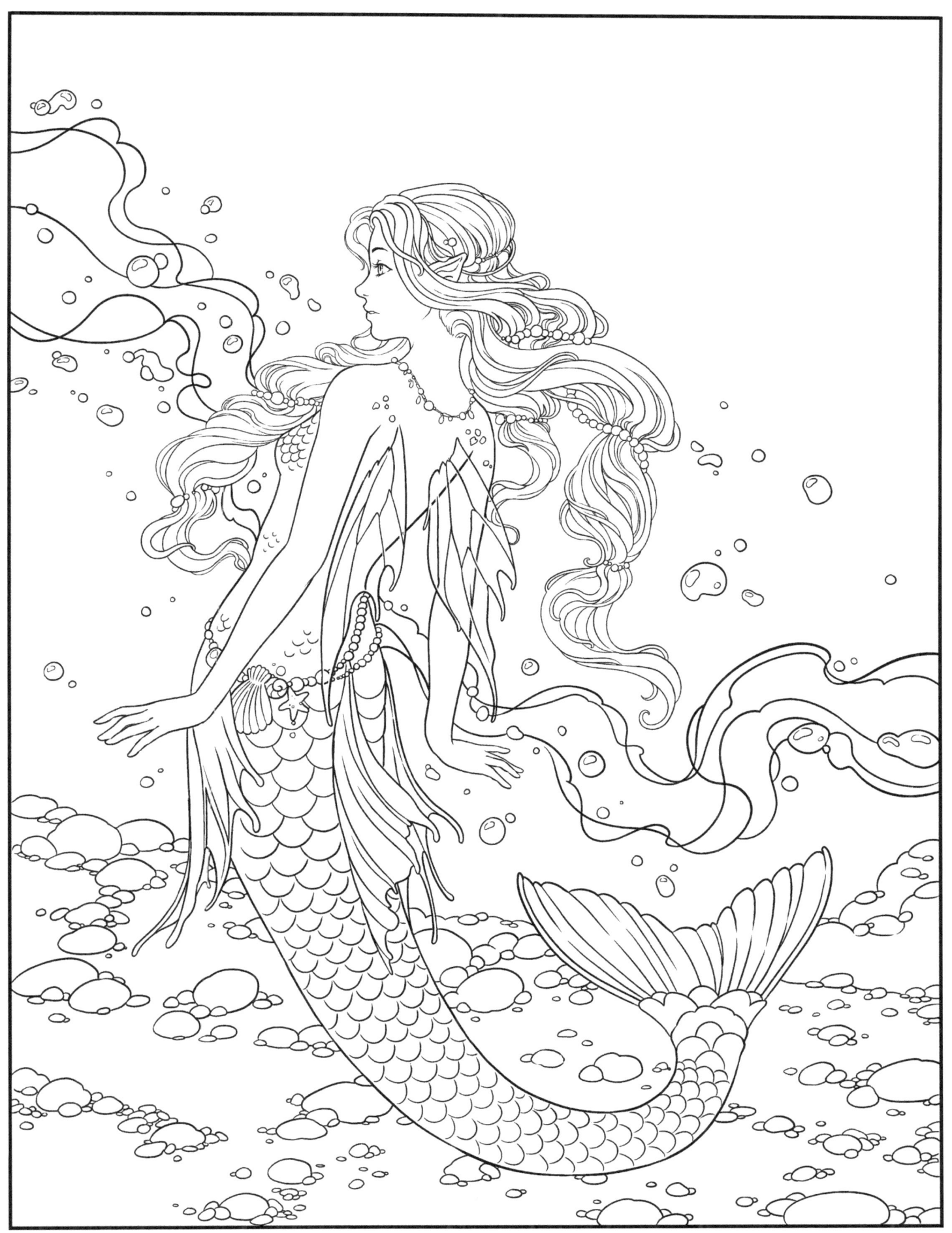

Previous Page: Shimmer
Lineart by Meredith Dillman

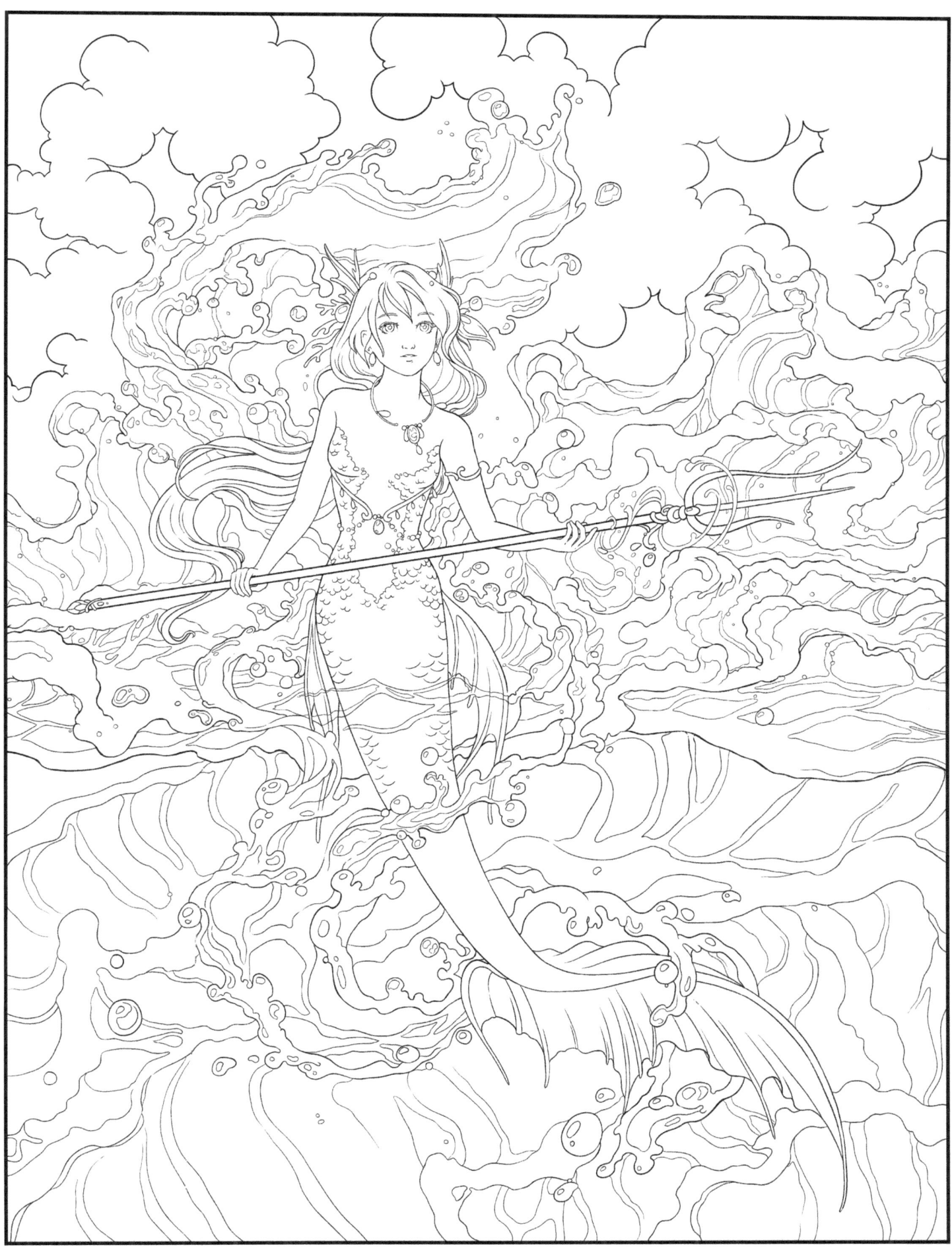

Previous Page: Protector of the Sea
Lineart by Meredith Dillman

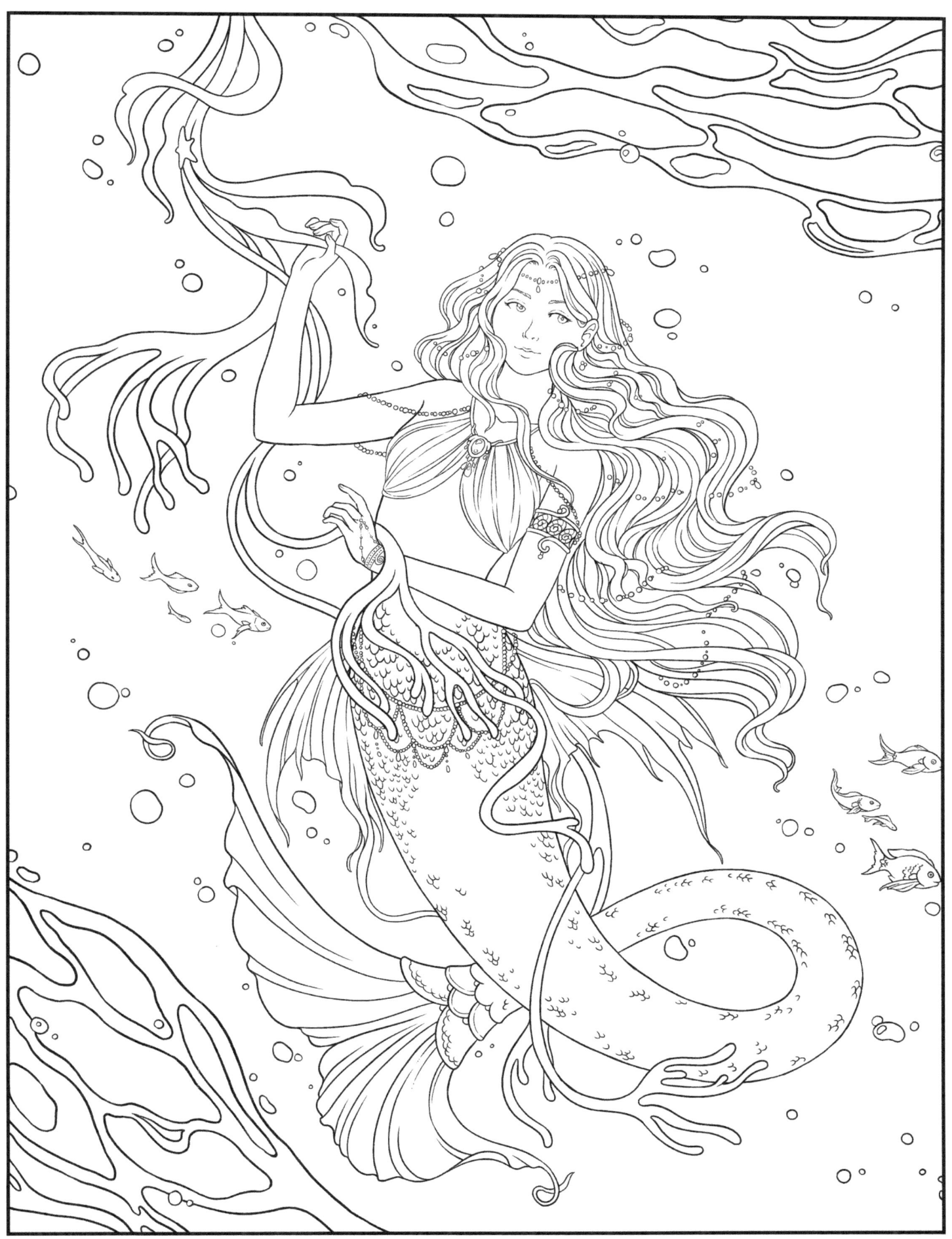

Previous Page: Among the Seaweed
Lineart by Meredith Dillman

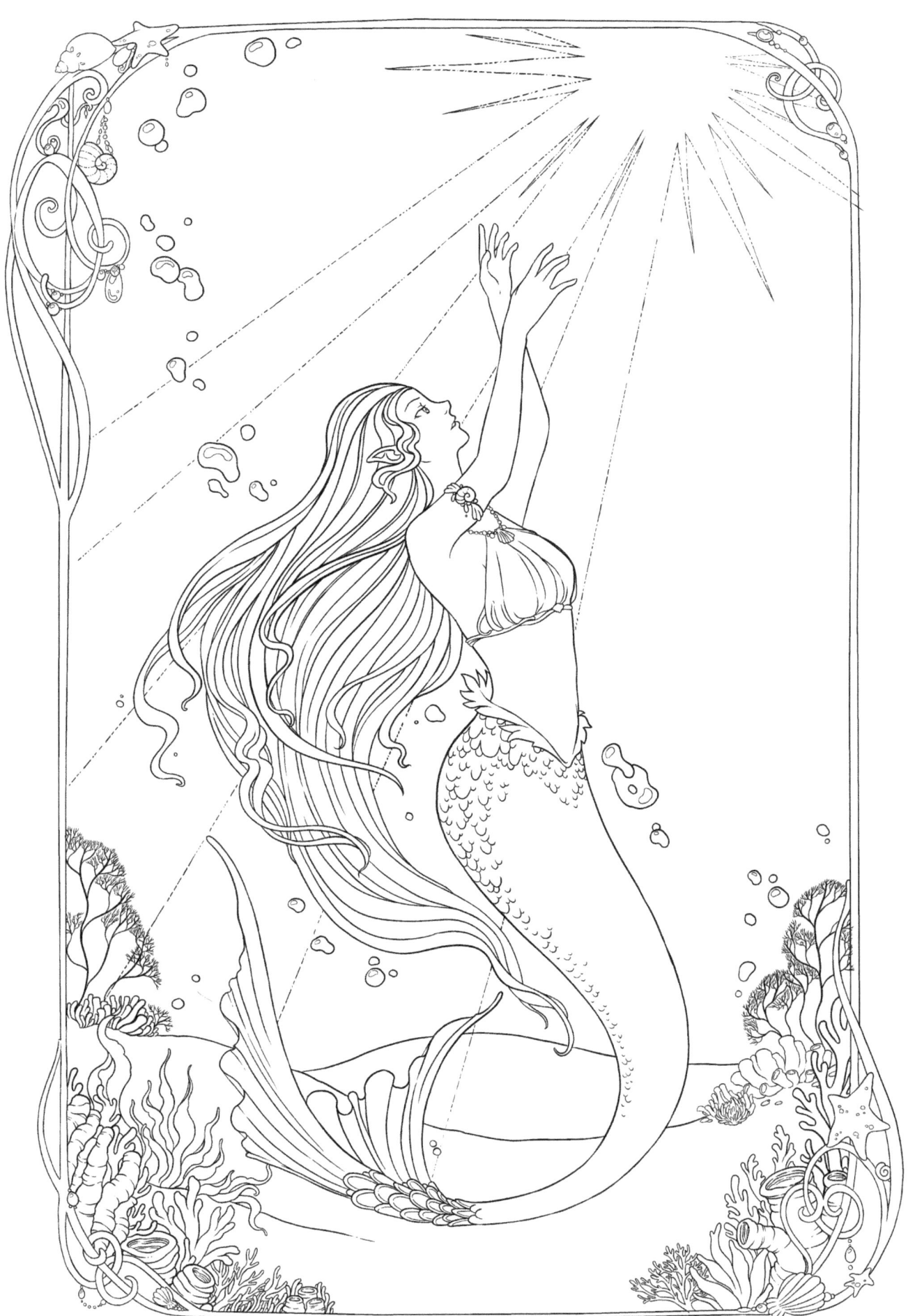

Previous Page: Reaching Sunlight
Lineart by Meredith Dillman

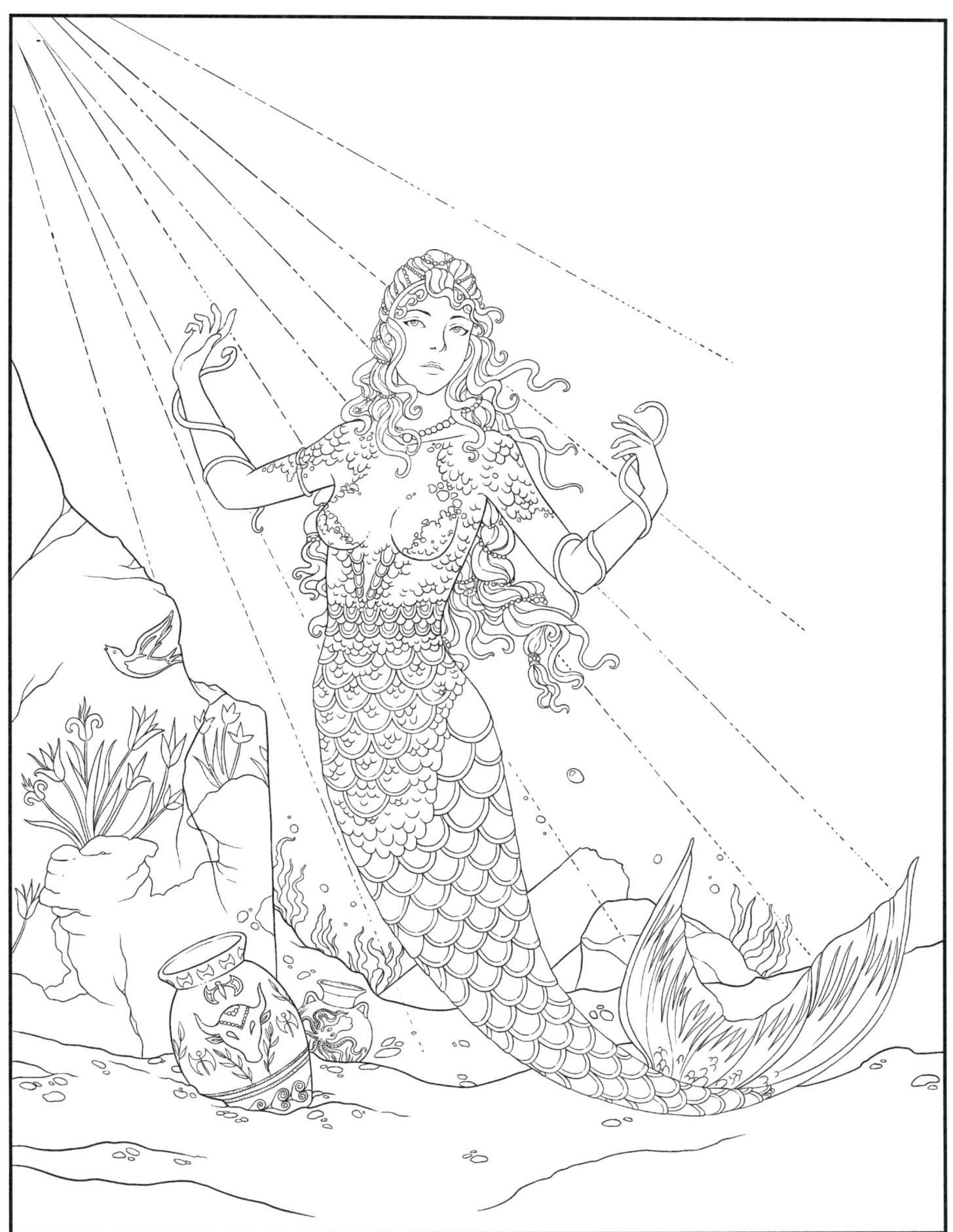

Previous Page: Minoan Mermaid
Lineart by Meredith Dillman